NDSHIRE
th
TANFORD her
ur Newely deſcribed.

STANFORD

A Scale of Paſes
50 100 150 200

Part   of

Lin

coln

Shire

EAST

Stretfo wood
Lithcall wood
Clipsham
Stretton
Greetham
OE
Yauldal wood
Fiue mille croſſe
Croſe mill
Tarringley wood
Hardwick
Exton
Horne
Horneimill
UND
Empingham wood
St Botulphe
NT
Empingham
Whitwell

Oſburneall wood
Newall wood
Pickeworth
Wolfyky wood
Turnecouſe wood
Woodhead wood
Friſh wood
Eſt wood
Beyal weed
Empingam wood
Tikencote
Ingthorp
Caſterton
Bridge

Eſenden
Brokenell wood
Ryall
Belmsthorp
Thokthorp
Rullers Stone
Litle Caſterton

Wicheley   Heath

Normanton
Edyweſton
weſton wood
den
ED

Newboile
Ketten
Chater flu
Geeſton
Kelthorpe
Lefters Bridge

North: Luſſenham
Pylton
South Luſſenham
Tyxover
Moorecote
Barrugdon hey
Barroughden
Waggerley

Tymwell
Eaſton
Fregthorp
Celuweſton
Didington

PART

OF

SEMPER EADEM

Weland flu
Stanford
Burghley

NORTHAM:

WYKE HUNDRED
Haringrooth

TONSHYRE

THE   SCHALE   OF   MILES

With My Best Wishes,

Shi. T. Nowell.

Now & Then
RUTLAND

MULTUM · IN · PARVO

RUTLAND

Christine C. Nowell
& John J. Nowell

Foreword

In 1830 Thomas Moule, one of the most distinctive and best-loved of all the early Victorian mapmakers, assembled and published his superb collection of maps in his book 'The English Counties'. He described Rutlandshire as; 'The smallest county of England, 15 miles (24.1 kilometres) in length, and 11 miles (17.7 kilometres) in breadth. It is bounded by Leicestershire, Nottinghamshire, Lincolnshire and Northamptonshire. It contains 48 parishes and two market towns. It yields good stone for building purposes. The air is very good, and the soil rich, producing excellent corn, and feeding a great number of cattle and sheep. The principal rivers are the Welland and the Gwash, or Wash. It is well wooded, and abounds in gentlemen's seat. Oakham, in the fertile Vale of Catmose, is the county town. It is pretty well built, has a free school and a hospital. It has a population of 2726, is 95 miles (152.86 kilometres) from London and has markets on Monday and Saturday. The total population of Rutlandshire is 21,302. It sends two members to parliament.'

This description paints a picture of a tranquil time when stately, ancestral country houses were filled with weekend visitors, often including Royal hunting parties. A time when elaborately decorated, well-established parish churches were filled with devout congregations. When country towns had busy streets and market places, and picturesque villages filled a landscape that offered 'scenes, situations and prospects remarkable for their extent and beauty.' An idyllic time for the rich but undoubtedly, not so idyllic for the common man.

In the 1830's, with the industrial revolution sweeping across the country, there was an ever-growing need for travel and transportation. Horse drawn coaches and carriages sped along the newly developed turnpikes; canals were dug for the graceful barges that carried cargo between towns and villages; railways arrived in a flourish of steam and conflict, and later flying machines descended from the skies. Wars were fought and won. The 'Rutland Volunteers' had already fought bravely in the Boer Wars on the Northwest Frontier. Then came the 'Great War' - the war to end all wars. The men of Rutland went in, proportionally, greater numbers than from any other county to fight and die on foreign soil. Peace returned for a while and life ebbed and flowed for the people of Rutland until, in the 1980s, inevitable changes came about. Major decisions were made, and despite much protest, homes and villages were lost and Rutland Water slowly filled a landscape that was to change forever. Tourists and numerous new residents arrived, attracted by both the rural charm and central location of this picturesque and enchanting county. With increasing numbers came demands for new services, which in turn led to the loss of many fine artefacts of historic Rutland. In the headlong race towards 'progress', many irreplaceable buildings simply disappeared without a significant memorial, a great loss for all of those who know and love Rutland. Within these pages, historic happenings and locations are displayed, some, fortunately still preserved, others sadly lost. But the final triumph is that whatever happens to Rutland, this smallest but most English of counties, 'Multum in Parvo' - much in little - will forever describe it and its people.

Councillor David Richardson,
Catmose,
Oakham,
The County of Rutland.

Now & Then
RUTLAND

By Christine C. Nowell
Photography by John J. Nowell FRGS LRPS

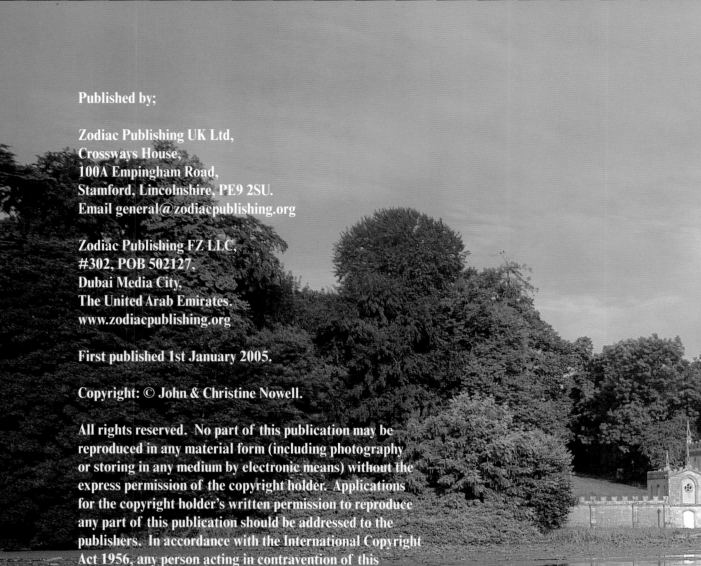

Published by;

Zodiac Publishing UK Ltd,
Crossways House,
100A Empingham Road,
Stamford, Lincolnshire, PE9 2SU.
Email general@zodiacpublishing.org

Zodiac Publishing FZ LLC,
#302, POB 502127,
Dubai Media City,
The United Arab Emirates.
www.zodiacpublishing.org

First published 1st January 2005.

Other books in the series and by the author:

A Day Above Yemen
A Day Above Oman
A Day Above The Emirates
A Day Above Sri Lanka

Now & Then - Bahrain
Now & Then - The Emirates
Now & Then - Abu Dhabi
Now & Then - Sharjah
Now & Then - Dubai (English & German)
Now & Then - Oman (English & German)

ISBN 1- 904566 - 09 - X
LCCN 2003105982

Design by Stephen Varty for Zodiac Publishing UK Ltd.
Scanning by gildenburgh media solutions, Peterborough.
Separations & printing by Butler & Tanner, Frome, UK.

Contents

Cover: Oakham Castle with All Saints Church in the background.

Page 1: A County of Rutland horse-brass photographed on a typical piece of 'ironstone' rock. 'Multum In Parvo' translates as 'Much In Little'.

Pages 2/3: In the brief time before sunset, the rippled, glassy waterscape on the southern shore of Rutland Water reflects Normanton Church. The longest river in Rutland, the Gwash, flows into this lake.

Pages 4/5: Fort Henry overlooks the ornamental lakes on the Exton Estate which were built hundreds of years ago, primarily to dam water to irrigate crops and establish the fish ponds to provide a varied diet for the landowners.

Pages 6/7: Burley House dominates the view from every corner of Rutland. The house was originally built in 1724. Inset: The Finch Family on the steps of the main house in 1880. Inset: In 1908, a fire started in the house in the early hours of the morning. One of the occupants was Mr. Winston Churchill who, with typical leadership, organised the rescue of several residents. He was dressed in his pyjamas with a bath towel around his middle, which kept slipping down. Mr Lane, the postman, renowned for delivering the mail by cart, donkey and even a retired Grand National winner, arrived on the scene and produced a large horse shoe nail which was used to secure the towel. The gallant, local fire brigade arrived but was unable to save much of the house and the assembled audience watched as molten lead poured from the roof.

Pages 8/9: The Rutland Belle, the largest vessel on Rutland Water. Inset: Boating in the late 18th Century on the Barrowden millpond fed by the River Welland.

Pages 10/11: The Railway Inn at Geeston was the subject of the master photographer, Mr. Charles Henton, on the 12th August 1915. The road runs down past the Inn and the impressive 13th Century Church to a bridge, which crosses the River Chater.

Introduction

Rutland is said to be the most English of all the English counties. It has the unique distinction of being the smallest county in England and whilst its scenery is neither magnificent nor grand, it does possess that peaceful, pastoral charm so characteristic of rural England. From the county's highest vantage points around Uppingham and Ridlington, the rolling hills and dales, pastures and woodlands, streams and coppices can be seen to stretch far into the distance. The plateau to the north is more highly cultivated, with large wooded areas whilst the southern half of the county consists of a series of ridges running east to west, interspersed with valleys of rich pasture land. The view of the Vale of Catmose approaching the county town of Oakham inspired the poet Drayton to write:

'Bring forth that British vale, and be it ne'er so rare,
But Catmus with that vale for richness may compare.'
'O Catmus, thou fair vale! Come on in grass and corn
That Beaver ne'er be said they sisterhood to scorn.
And let thy Ocham boast to have no little grace
That her the pleased Fates did in they bosom place!'

Rutland is situated almost in the centre of England, surrounded by the larger counties of Lincolnshire, Leicestershire and Northamptonshire. The county covers a heart-shaped area of approximately 150 sq. miles, measuring some 38 miles across at its widest point, east to west, and approximately 17 miles from north to south. The river Welland forms Rutland's southern border, dividing it from Northamptonshire, whilst in the southwest the Eye Brook separates it from Leicestershire. Two other rivers, the Gwash and Chater, flow into the county before joining the Welland, which in turn discharges into the Wash. A small part of Lincolnshire protrudes into Rutland on the eastern side, just west of the town of Stamford and approximately 12 miles of the old Great North Road (known in Roman times as Ermine Street and now know as the A1), crosses the top northern corner of the county.

We do not know for certain how the county came to be known as Rutland. Some say that the ancient name of 'Roteland' was given to this area because of the dark red colour of the soil. Others claim that the land may have once belonged to someone of that name. However the name came about we do know that the rocks underlying the soil of Rutland date back to Jurassic and Pleistocene times. The most valuable, from an industrial point of view, is the excellent building stone of the Oolite formation, which is still quarried at Ketton, Edith Weston, Casterton and Clipsham. Ironstone is quarried at Cottesmore and Market Overton. These Jurassic rocks have a considerable dip to the eastward, and this combined with the action of rain and water, accounts for its undulating appearance.

Whilst little is known of life in the pre-historic Rutland, an almost complete skeleton of a Cetiosaurus, unearthed at Great Casterton in 1968, indicates that the area was once a large river estuary, where plant eating dinosaurs grazed. Long after the dinosaurs became extinct, early Man arrived in Rutland and findings suggest that he used a site on a hilltop near Glaston as a look out. These Mesolithic hunters stalked their game and their successes yielded a variety of remains that have recently been unearthed. The oldest were mammoth and 'woolly' rhinoceros bones dating from the end of the last Ice Age. Humans were using stone axes, characteristic of the Mesolithic period, 5,000-6,000 years ago and several such axes have been found in the northern part of the county. Surprisingly one was made of stone from the Langdale Valley in the Lake District indicating that man indulged in travel and perhaps trade even in those early days. In 1906 a Bronze Age hoard of craftsmen's tools was unearthed at the Cottesmore ironstone workings and a number of bronze socketed axes were found at Ketton dating back some 3,000-4,000 years. Tantalising clues to life in those early days.

History moved on and the Romans moved in. The land that had previously been home to the tribe known as the Coritani became part of the Roman province known as Flavia Caesariensis. Remains of several villas and a fort have been discovered at Great Casterton and Market Overton indicating that the Romans not only passed through the area on their way north, but also chose to settle here. The Romans were famous for their magnificent roads and Ermine Street, built to connect London and Lincoln and now part of the A1, is a lasting reminder of their presence. After the Romans left other invaders arrived, including the Anglo Saxons and later, the Norsemen, to leave their mark on country and county. Recent findings at North Luffenham, Cottesmore and Market Overton suggest that they may have been important Anglo Saxon settlements in the 5th and 6th centuries. The discoveries found at North Luffenham consisted of spearheads, knives, shield -bosses, urns, bronze ornaments and glass beads, these are now housed in the County Museum. Later still Norsemen were to invade both England and France. It was through his ancestral connection to these invading forces that William of France claimed his right to the English throne. William's defeat of the English King at the Battle of Hastings in 1066 AD was yet another major turning point in the history of England.

By the time of the Norman Conquest every village that is now in the county of Rutland and some that have since been lost, had been founded. The county itself did not exist as a separate entity. In the Domesday Book, an accounting of England ordered by William after his conquest, the area was recorded for tax purposes as part of its neighbouring shires with no reference to the name 'Roteland'. We know that Edward the Confessor bequeathed 'Roteland' to his wife Edith for her life and afterwards, in 1064, to his newly founded Abbey of St Peter at Westminster. The village of Edith Weston is named after Queen Edith and the second part of the name suggests that there may have been other royal land to the east. Although not designated as a separate shire or a county it is apparent that the area of Roteland was royal hunting land traditionally gifted as a dowry.

The first written mention of Rutland was in 1155 when a Sheriff of Rutland was first noted. Rutland was first mentioned as a county when in 1204, King John,

following royal tradition gave in dowry, the county of Rutland, made up of part of Northamptonshire and Nottinghamshire, to his wife, Queen Isabella.

Following the Norman Conquest much of the land was owned by the de Brus family, passing by marriage to the Haringtons in the early 16th century. At that time the Haringtons were the most important family in Rutland. The most powerful member of the family was Sir John Harington, created Baron Harington at the coronation of King James I of England. This elevation became a mixed blessing when he was made guardian and tutor of James' daughter, Elizabeth. Princess Elizabeth spent some time at Lord Harington's home at Exton and the avenue of trees leading to the gatehouse at the entrance to Exton Park, is said to have been her favourite walk and is named after her. Without a suitable allowance the high cost of entertaining Elizabeth ruined the baron. He minted his own money, made of brass, but this was turned out to be valueless, which lead to the saying "not worth a brass farthing". The princess married the Elector Palatine to become "Queen of Bohemia". Lord Harington accompanied her to Bohemia, but died in 1613 on his way back to England. After his death, the estate was sold to pay his creditors, and was purchased by Sir Baptist Hicks. His daughter married the 1st Baron Noel; the Noel family took over the estate and has kept it to this day. Sir Baptist Hicks purchased another estate, Campden in Gloucestershire, and was later created Viscount Campden. The present Viscount Campden lives in Exton Hall.

By the 13th century the 'Forest of Rutland' was extensive and used as a Royal Hunting Preserve under strict 'Forest Laws'. Much of Rutland was answerable to these often harsh and unjust forest laws overseen by a Chief Forester. Royal interest in these hunting lands diminished by the 15 century and it became more attractive to rent or sell these lands for additional income. The size of the forest diminished and it eventually became more generally known as 'Leighfield Forest', probably named after the manor situated at the centre of the area. Wardley Wood, Beaumont Chase and Stoke Wood are survivals of the old 'Forest of Rutland.'

During the Wars of the Roses in the 15th century, Rutland played a conspicuous part in our national history when it was the scene of a battle, which had far reaching results. This was the Battle of Empingham fought near the Great North Road in 1470. The leader of the insurgents was Sir Robert Welles and the successes he met with at the outset were sufficient to alarm King Edward IV. The King marched north with his armies reaching Stamford on 11th March 1470. The following day the King made Lord Willoughby, Welles' father, whom he had brought with him from London as a hostage, write a letter to his son calling upon him to disperse his troops, but this was refused. Edward beheaded Lord Willoughby, in sight of his son's army. When the attack was made, the result was never in doubt and the insurgent forces were soon in full flight. Many of the fugitives fled casting away their distinguishing coats in the hopes of escaping unseen, hence the name, 'the Battle of Losecoat Field'.

The early 19th Century saw the opening of the Oakham and Melton Canal. Construction had begun on Oakham Canal, in response to threat of a French invasion, so that both goods and troops could be moved around the countryside more quickly. The canal was finally opened in 1802. Wharves were situated at Saxby, Stapleford, Market Overton, Cottesmore and Oakham. The advantage of transporting goods and people by canal was rapidly over taken by the introduction of the railway. By the mid 1800s railway lines criss-crossed Rutland, connecting villages and the market towns of Oakham and Uppingham, enabling people to travel and goods to be moved about the county with ever-increasing ease.

The story of this book begins with the advent of the railway as a new means of travel and photography as a new means of recording images. Both, at the time, as revolutionary a means of communication as the mobile phone is today. The new railway travellers wanted to communicate with those at home and in 1869 the first postcard appeared in Austria. At first these cards were not illustrated but by 1894 the postal authorities allowed photographs to be printed on one side of the card and this led to the birth of a new industry - postcard production. Photographers published pictures on card depicting local scenes and in 1911 alone, over 2,000,000 postcards were posted every day. The international craze for postcards and mail in general spread throughout the British Empire to such an extent that in 1936 Imperial Airways ordered an entire fleet of Empire flying boats whose primary purpose was to deliver mail to the Dominions.

In Rutland the many new amateur photographers and the more highly skilled professionals, such as Charles Henton, captured the county and its people on film for the first time. This has lead, some 100 years later, to another development, that of the postcard collector. Some of these old cards are unique and priceless, others are less valuable. One thing they all have in common is that they capture moments in history that would otherwise be lost to us today. In turn, the availability of these old images has inspired the comparative aspects of this 'Now & Then' series of books. As we rush headlong through the 21st century, with all that new technology has to offer, there is an increasing interest in how things used to be. For the older residents of Rutland, perhaps the most recent dramatic changes were the flooding of the valleys and the demise of Rutland as a county. The flooding produced the vast expanse of the appropriately, horseshoe-shaped, Rutland Water.

Although vigorously opposed, Rutland was briefly reduced to a district of Leicestershire, however, in 1994, after a sustained campaign, Rutland was returned to County status. There have been momentous changes but, despite such events, some of the scenes pictured in this book are timeless, others have changed beyond recognition, but most importantly this book is a record of how things were and how they are today.

Christine C. Nowell
Oakham
Rutland

Chapter 1
The History of Rutland

THE RUTLAND DINOSAUR, NOW DISPLAYED in Leicester City Museum, was found near Great Casterton in 1968. The dinosaur is the most complete example of a Cetiosaurus ever found. Little further evidence of early life in Rutland has been found until Roman times when the conquest of the country began with the Roman invasion in AD. 49. The Romans built a fort, the remains can still be seen to this day, at Great Casterton. About 100 AD, the Romans expanded the town at Great Casterton and additional farms were needed to supply the town with food. Evidence of villas and settlements have been found at Market Overton, Thistleton, Tinwell, Glaston, Tixover, Empingham and Whitwell. With changing circumstances, the Romans built a defensive circuit of walls around the town at Great Casterton about 350 AD. By 410 AD, the Romans had left to be replaced by other invaders; the Angles, Saxons and Jutes from Northern Germany and Jutland. Around 430 AD, the original Roman town at Great Casterton was destroyed by fire. One of the major Roman roads, Ermine Street, passed through Great Casterton or Casterton Magna, as it was then known, to connect London with Lincoln and York. Although it has always been a busy major route, the monochrome photograph shows a man with his wheelbarrow standing in the road, just outside the Crown Inn where the famous highwayman, Dick Turpin, is reputed to have lodged. Unique examples of old working agricultural machines and traction engines are also preserved in the village and, in conjunction with the society of ploughmen, are demonstrated every year in a working weekend.

In 1066, WILLIAM THE CONQUEROR DEFEATED King Harold at the Battle of Hastings. In 1086, he ordered the famous survey of his new possession, England. Although the Domesday Book is a complete record of the country it does not specifically mention Rutland but rather divided the area into two, one part accountable to Nottinghamshire the other to Northamptonshire. The first mention of the county name is in records of the Sheriff of Rutland in 1155. Walkelin de Ferrers built the Great Hall of Oakham Castle about 1190; his emblem was the now familiar Rutland horseshoe. The custom of distinguished visitors to the castle surrendering a horseshoe to the Lord of the Manor probably dates from this time. King John gave Rutland to his wife Isabella in 1204 as a dowry in accordance with ancient custom. King John also visited Oakham Castle in 1204, which served as a base for hunting in the Forest of Rutland. From 1219 to 1258, Henry III was a frequent visitor to Oakham Castle and granted the Manor of Oakham to his younger brother Richard, Earl of Cornwall. During this period, in 1229, the First Assize Courts were held at Oakham Castle. Tinwell, with its distinctive forge, was famous for its cloths, which were sold in Stamford.

THE BATTLE OF EMPINGHAM, ALSO known as the Battle of Losecoat Field, took place on the 12th March 1470 during the Wars of the Roses. King Edward had left London to join his army being mustered near Grantham to put down the rebellion led by Sir Robert Welles. King Edward held Welles's father captive and the two forces assembled for battle at a location adjacent to the present day A1 still called Bloody Oaks. Edward executed Welles's father in front of the rebels and they, the rebels, advanced. Edward fired his canons and then charged and the battle turned into a rout against the Lancastrians. Some of the rebels, led by the Squire of Pickworth, Sir John Hussey, retreated to Pickworth discarding their coats bearing his colours - hence the name, 'Losecoat Field'. A battle ensued within the village, which was destroyed, just one arch of the old church left standing as a reminder. 10,000 men were said to have been killed in the battle and workmen digging near the site found a mass grave containing the bones of many young men. 400 years ago, Guy Fawkes hatched a plan to blow up the houses of Parliament. A local worthy, Sir Edward Digby, one of Guy Fawkes' fellow-conspirators, had an estate at Stoke Dry. There is a tradition that a room over the north porch of the village church was the birthplace of the Gunpowder Plot, but this does not bear investigation. Today, both Empingham and Stoke Dry are tranquil spots.

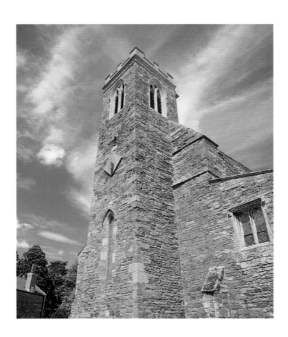

CALDECOTT IS SITUATED AT THE MOST
southerly part of Rutland where Eye Brook and
the River Welland meet. The Romans used a
ford, located here since ancient times. Adjacent
to the ford was a small patch of grass where the
villagers could bleach their own hand-spun and
hand-woven linen. Here at the natural crossing,
a narrow bridge was built on the main coach route
from the south. This bridge was damaged when
a traction engine went through it into the water.
As the industrial revolution got underway in the
late 1700s, the age of the great canals came and
went. While abroad, the French Revolution was

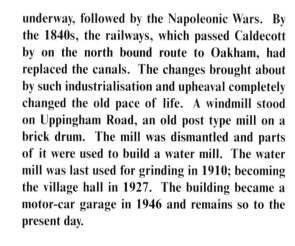

underway, followed by the Napoleonic Wars. By the 1840s, the railways, which passed Caldecott by on the north bound route to Oakham, had replaced the canals. The changes brought about by such industrialisation and upheaval completely changed the old pace of life. A windmill stood on Uppingham Road, an old post type mill on a brick drum. The mill was dismantled and parts of it were used to build a water mill. The water mill was last used for grinding in 1910; becoming the village hall in 1927. The building became a motor-car garage in 1946 and remains so to the present day.

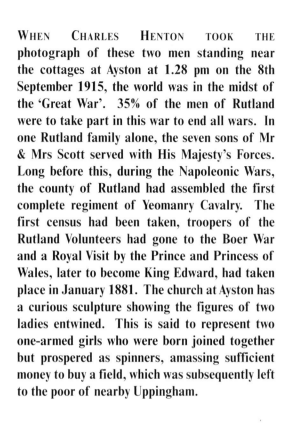

WHEN CHARLES HENTON TOOK THE photograph of these two men standing near the cottages at Ayston at 1.28 pm on the 8th September 1915, the world was in the midst of the 'Great War'. 35% of the men of Rutland were to take part in this war to end all wars. In one Rutland family alone, the seven sons of Mr & Mrs Scott served with His Majesty's Forces. Long before this, during the Napoleonic Wars, the county of Rutland had assembled the first complete regiment of Yeomanry Cavalry. The first census had been taken, troopers of the Rutland Volunteers had gone to the Boer War and a Royal Visit by the Prince and Princess of Wales, later to become King Edward, had taken place in January 1881. The church at Ayston has a curious sculpture showing the figures of two ladies entwined. This is said to represent two one-armed girls who were born joined together but prospered as spinners, amassing sufficient money to buy a field, which was subsequently left to the poor of nearby Uppingham.

ROGER DE KETTON WAS BORN IN THE village of Ketton in 1143 AD. He grew up to be a scholar and went on to be a translator, mathematician, alchemist and the Dean of Pamplona Cathedral in Navarre, Spain. At the time, the Crusades were at their height. Despite Muslims being thought of as the enemy, Roger de Ketton translated Muslim scientific discoveries in alchemy and algebra (both Arabic words) into Latin, the language of European scholars. He also went on to translate the Koran into Latin and his books were the first to reach Europe on these subjects. Centuries later, science was again focused onto Ketton when the cement works were established in 1928. Over the past 80 years, the process of making cement has been refined and improved with old methods, including the old chimney-stacks, being replaced by new technology. Today, Ketton Works is a large modern cement plant that has both local and national economic significance. Its roots are in the combination of the desire of modern society to have a comfortable and effectively built environment and the local availability of the key raw material, limestone. The impact of the company's operations arises from the very nature of cement production involving quarrying, large-scale industrial production and national distribution using road and rail. Cement is an essential component of the built environment. Without it, we would have no schools, hospitals or homes.

Chapter 2
Agriculture
& Windmills

THE MAINSTAY OF THE INDUSTRIAL revolution in Great Britain was the surplus food production, which was provided by agricultural counties such as Rutland where the sweeping expanse of cornfields was interspersed by towering windmills. The first windmills date from the 12th Century but illustrations only became available from the 14th Century. The simplest type of windmill was the 'post mill'; so-called after the large post on which the main structure of the mill is balanced. Whissendine is a 'Smock' mill where the improved design allowed the rotatable cap, which held the sails, wind shaft and brake wheel to move independently of the main body of the mill. This meant that the fixed wooden or stone body could be larger, housing more grinding stones and machinery. It could also be taller, have longer sails and hence catch more wind. Mr Nigel Moon has spent several years renovating the Whissendine mill and today it produces the finest organic flour. The renovations will continue and it is planned that the mill will once again display its four sails.

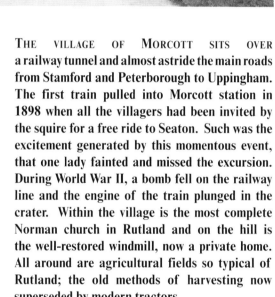

THE VILLAGE OF MORCOTT SITS OVER a railway tunnel and almost astride the main roads from Stamford and Peterborough to Uppingham. The first train pulled into Morcott station in 1898 when all the villagers had been invited by the squire for a free ride to Seaton. Such was the excitement generated by this momentous event, that one lady fainted and missed the excursion. During World War II, a bomb fell on the railway line and the engine of the train plunged in the crater. Within the village is the most complete Norman church in Rutland and on the hill is the well-restored windmill, now a private home. All around are agricultural fields so typical of Rutland; the old methods of harvesting now superseded by modern tractors.

THE BROAD EXPANSE OF MODERN cultivated land stretches towards Ridlington. When Henton took his picture in the village, on the 24th August 1915, he could not have imagined that the scene would be unchanged almost 100 years later. Ridlington was once a major village at the edge of Leighfield Forest, part of the extensive Royal Deer Park that existed to the west of the village. No road progresses beyond the village and isolated farms with names such as Park Farm and Park Lodge are reminders of the once-extensive forest and park. The last stag of Leighfield Forest was hunted and caught in Russell's paddock in 1800. Long before that, in 1605, Sir James Harrington, of the old Hall, was responsible for organising the delivery of French gunpowder for the Gunpowder Plot and the horses needed for the final getaway. Once the forest was cleared, horse-drawn ploughs broke up the land and today, combine harvesters sweep down the slopes.

THE POET, DAVID HOPE, DESCRIBED the abandoned windmill of South Luffenham:

'Long since the mill was built to last,
Part of a changeless scene,
For still the clouds go sailing past,
And still the fields are green,
Many men have come and gone,
Cared for the land and passed it on.'

In the village, Henton took this photograph on the 16th June 1916, late in the afternoon at 5.30 pm, when the sun was casting dark shadows across the street towards the public house. Within St Marys' Church, in the south aisle, is a slab of marble commemorating the death of a Princess of the Romanies. During Christmas 1793, a tribe of gypsies and their 'King' called Edward Baswell, were camped near the bridge called the 'Follies'. The King's daughter, Princess Rose, lay dying of tuberculosis, known in those days as consumption. When she died, the villagers refused to allow her to be buried in the churchyard. The Vicar, however, decreed that the Princess would be buried within the church under his jurisdiction and over 20,000 Romanies attended the funeral. The ghost of an old lady, who only appears after arguments within the pub, haunts the Boot & Shoe Inn. During World War II, when all the men had gone off to the war, the so-called army of land girls ploughed the land and rode the farm horses.

THE STATELY PROGRESS OF A COMBINE HARVESTER descends the slope of red soil towards the village of Bisbrooke, leading away from the busy main road between Peterborough and nearby Uppingham. The first written record of Rutland occurred in 863 AD, as 'Roteland', the land of red soil. Rutland did not exist as a county until almost three hundred years later when it was constituted from two wapentakes, detached from the sheriffdom of Nottingham and part of Northamptonshire. King John presented the resulting county to Queen Isabella. The old Roteland had belonged to other royal ladies, first to the mother of Ethelred the Unready and then to his queen, Emma. The Gate Inn was originally built as a farmhouse but was converted into a pub when the railway was being built.

BELTON-IN-RUTLAND WAS RE-NAMED BY HIS Grace, the Duke of Rutland to avoid confusion with the other villages of the same name in Leicestershire and the Midlands. Belton means 'village in the glade' and is a reflection of its ancient position within the great Royal Forest of Leighfield. Belton once held a substantial 3-day fair and was once on the main route between Leicester and Uppingham, which later became a turnpike and major coach route. Legend has it that Charles I rested here on the King's Stone following his defeat at the battle of Naseby. The stone base of the war Memorial, the bottom step of the original cross, is still known as the King's Stone. Almost all the village was destroyed by fire in 1776. Only a few of the original 17th and 18th century ironstone houses still exist.

Chapter 3
Roads, Canals & Railways

IN 1753, THE FIRST TURNPIKE TRUST was established in Rutland to build a road from Nottingham via Oakham and Uppingham to Kettering. In the same year the turnpike road from Stamford to Leicester via Uppingham was finished. Others soon followed; Stamford to Oakham via Empingham and Oakham to the Great North Road via Greetham. Regular coach and mail services were established. Mail was collected and delivered and fresh horses provided by various inns along the route. The children shown on the monochrome photograph, taken in 1914, used the road outside the Langham village school as a playground. This was, and still is the main road between Oakham and Melton Mowbray and was used by the London to Nottingham and Leeds coaches in the early 18th Century. The northbound coach would have changed horses at the George Hotel, now called the Whipper Inn, in Oakham's market square. The next change of horses would have taken place at Melton Mowbray. By 1830, there were more than 500 coaches covering some 12,000 miles (19,308 kilometres) of turnpikes employing more than 30,000 men and a staggering 150,000 horses. But the shadow of steam-driven rail engines came on the scene. The first commercial railway line had opened between Stockton and Darlington in 1825 and in 1839 alone, 5 million people travelled between London and Birmingham. The age of the coach came to an end and today, at the Whipper Inn, the stable block has now been converted into bedrooms surrounded by colourful hanging baskets. In 1858, a brewery moved to Langham, near Oakham and in 1911 it was bought by George Ruddle. The Ruddle family brewed at Langham until the 1980s and their ales became synonymous with Rutland. Today, the modern view shows the same school building, now a private house, which fronts onto the busy A606 road.

HENTON TOOK HIS SPLENDID PHOTOGRAPH of Ashwell church on a clear autumn morning at 11.29 am on the 30th October 1913. In the churchyard is the grave of Reverend J.W. Adams V.C. who is the only vicar ever to be awarded the Victoria Cross. Lord Roberts recommended the citation for his bravery in rescuing wounded soldiers from a river whilst under continuous fire. He served on the North West Frontier between Afghanistan and India (now Pakistan). He died in 1903, almost 100 years after the 15-mile canal, built in the late 17th Century, was finally opened in 1802. The canal, with its 18 locks, circled Ashwell and Barrow on its route between Melton and Oakham. The canal ended behind the Odd House Pub and 'Wharflands', part of Oakham School, is built on the site. The canal was designed to be part of the Leicester to Stamford canal but the connection between Oakham and Stamford was never built. By the 1830s, the railways were developing rapidly which proved to be the death knell of the canal and it finally closed in October 1847. The Stamford - Oakham - Melton section of the Midland railway opened on 20th March 1848. Today, large sections of the canal are still visible; some still filled with water and good fishing.

IN THE EARLY **1800**S, THE PACE OF RAILWAY construction was hectic. The two great railway companies, the London North Eastern Railway and the Midland Railway joined at Stamford with a further junction northeast of Preston where the line from Corby and Kettering met the line from Stamford, before the final run into Oakham. Charles Henton visited the village in 1914 to take his monochrome photograph. He found a pleasing village of limestone houses and the impressive 16th Century Manor House. The village is situated on the top of a rolling hill between Uppingham and Manton. A tunnel had to be built here before the final part of this line into Oakham could be finished. The Midland Railway Company originally built the signal box at Oakham in 1899. It is now very rare to see this type of signal box and this particular box was used for the design of a toy signal box, now a collector's item.

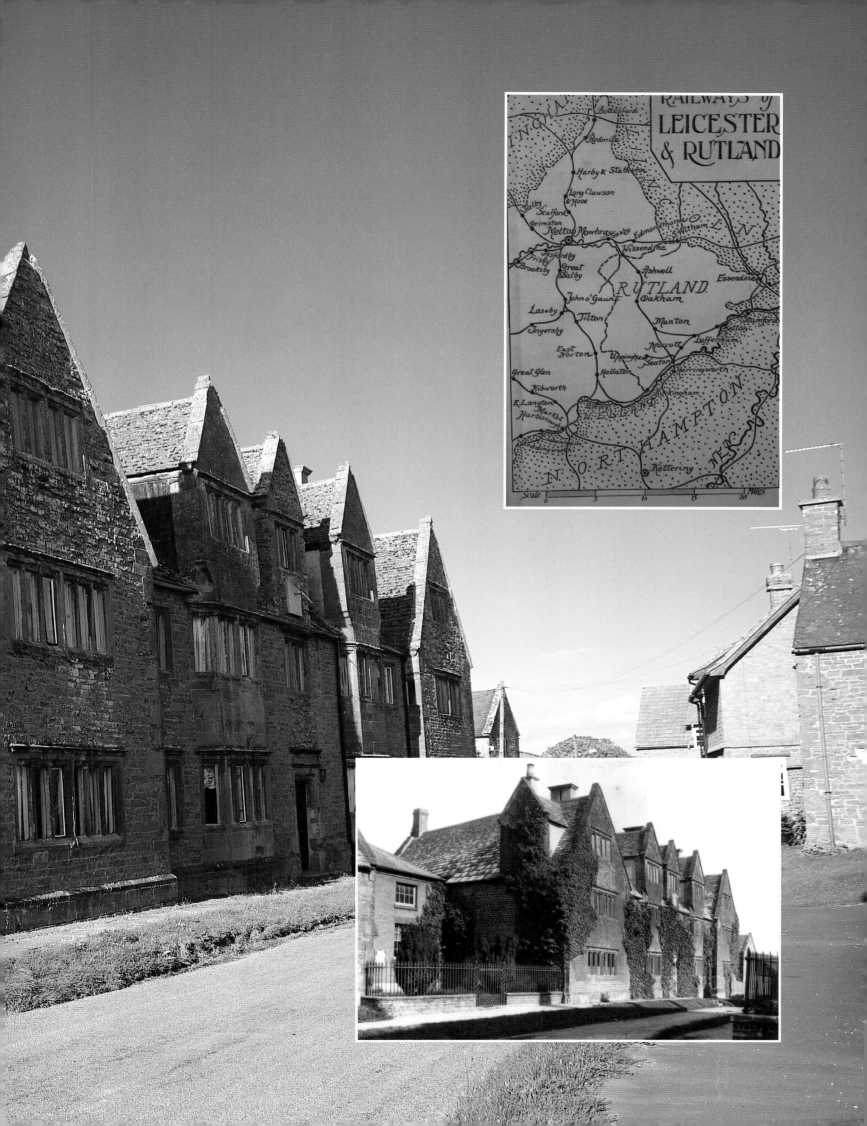

RAILWAYS of
LEICESTER
& RUTLAND

The tranquil view across the hidden Oakham-Stamford railway and the River Chater to Lyndon Hall has changed little since the railway was built and opened in 1848. Henton photographed Lyndon Hall in 1913. Today, the same viewpoint reveals that the north-eastern part of the Hall has been reconstructed. Behind the Hall, the clock tower and the stable block have also been carefully preserved. Lyndon Hall was opened in 1677 and in 1722 it was the birthplace of Thomas Barker, now known as 'the Father of English Meterology'. Thomas started keeping journals on the weather when he was just 11 years old and faithfully maintained his observations until he died on the 29th December 1809. His 65 years of weather observations are still referred to by the weathermen of today, in order to re-construct the weather patterns of those times. Behind the Hall is the restored church of St Martin, surrounded by tall, imposing pine trees. Although it is not open to the public, there are public footpaths all around the Hall to enable the visitor to catch a glimpse of this 'chocolate-box' scene.

ESSENDINE STILL RUMBLES TO THE PASSAGE OF express trains through the village but they do not stop here anymore. The Railway Hotel was built specifically for rail passengers and is still open for business today. The platforms at Essendine have long since disappeared but the World Speed Record for steam driven trains still stands. On the 3rd July 1938, the 'Mallard', designed by Sir Nigel Gresley, thundered through Essendine on its record-breaking run to reach 126 miles per hour (202.7 kilometres per hour). The 'Mallard', now preserved in the National Railway Museum at York, is a Gresley East Coast Pacific, originally belonging to the LNER class A4 4-6-2. The name 'Gresley' is taken from Sir Nigel Gresley, scion of an ancient family. He was appointed Locomotive Superintendent of the Great Northern Railway in 1911. He died in 1941, still in office, as Chief Mechanical Engineer. His reign saw remarkable developments in the railway world, the A4- being his most impressive design. The first A4 ran from London to Newcastle in 1935, by summer 1938 there were 35 in service and the last A4 was withdrawn from active service, after a remarkable career, in 1966. The A4's achieved a standard of spectacular performance and consistent reliability never surpassed by any other class of steam locomotive in the UK or the world.

ONE OF THE MOST SCENIC ROUTES IN THE MIDLANDS is the line from Kettering through Corby, Gretton, Harringworth, to Manton and Oakham. The old windmill at Seaton was probably built in the 1700s, long before a small army of 3,000 navvies, labourers from Ireland, built their camp on the flood plain to spend 3 years building the Seaton Viaduct for the Midland Railway Company. Their weekly pay was in the region of £1 5 shillings for labourers to £2 10 shillings for bricklayers. The viaduct, the last arch of which was keyed in 1878, carries the line for three-quarters of a mile (1.2 kilometers) on 82 arches averaging 57 feet in height. It crosses the river Welland and the now closed LNWR lines from Rugby to Peterborough, Seaton to Luffenham, and Seaton to Uppingham lines. The viaduct was built using an estimated 20 million bricks, made on site from local clay. It has been calculated that if the bricks were laid out side by side to form a pathway 63 inches wide it would stretch for 200 miles, equal to the distance from London to York. It was opened in 1878 and eventually closed to daily services in 1966. In the past few years, extensive restoration work has been carried out and on the 30th August 2004, the 'Union of South Africa', another of Sir Nigel Gresley' designs, made four crossings of the viaduct, carrying passengers. Plans are being developed to re-open this line from London to Oakham so that the public might enjoy this remarkable view once again.

ON THE 1ST NOVEMBER 1813, THIS VIEW OF THE village of Wardley would have shown a simple dirt road and an occasional cart or coach that would have to negotiate the slippery and muddy steep hill on the way to Uppingham. On the same day, the first balloon flight took place over Rutland. Mr Sadler flew 34 miles (54.7 kilometres) over Rutland and landed in the middle of Lord Lonsdale's hounds, which were out hunting at Pickworth. Almost 100 years later, the first aircraft flew over Rutland when a Bleriot monoplane piloted by Gustav Hamil landed in Uppingham in 1912. The Daily Mail 'Circuit of Britain' race took place later that year when one of the contestants, Mr C. P. Pizey, force landed his Bristol Biplane near Egleton but luckily was able to take off again after minor repairs. The reaction of the people of Rutland was one of joy and amazement. Only two years later, in 1916, a Zeppelin flew across Rutland dropping a stick of bombs between Sewstern and Thistleton, illuminated by a searchlight battery. Lt William Robinson RFC of Number 39 Squadron shot down the Zeppelin. Today, the bright red helicopter of the Air Ambulance Service stands by at East Midlands Airport ready to cover the region should any emergency arise.

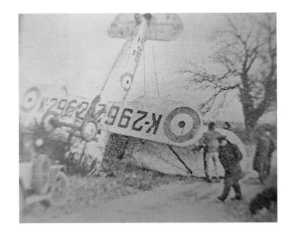

By the mid 1930s it was becoming obvious to the government that war was on the horizon and an urgent expansion programme commenced for the Royal Air Force. A secret survey was carried out on the well-drained limestone plateau around Cottesmore. Construction of RAF Cottesmore started in 1935 and the first aircraft, Vickers Wellesleys, plus one Fairey Battle, of number 35 & 207 Squadrons arrived in 1938. Both squadrons replaced all their Wellesley aircraft with Battles. The Fairey Battles took off from Cottesmore to join the Advanced Air Striking Force in France. They were to bomb the advancing German forces but suffered heavy losses. Other squadrons arrived with Hampden bombers and the Germans first bombed Cottesmore on 26th June 1940. 30 aircraft from Cottesmore took part in the first 1,000-bomber raid on 30th May 1942. On the 8th September 1943, the airfield was handed over to the American Army Air Corps who provided the aircrews to fly the ubiquitous Douglas Dakota carrying the paratroopers of the US 82nd Airborne Brigade. This quiet village has hardly changed since Charles Henton took his photograph in 1913 showing the wide-open road and mature trees. Worshippers around Rutland were disturbed just before 1100hrs on Sunday, the 17th September 1944 by the sound of the largest armada of aircraft ever to fly over Rutland, en-route to Arnhem for Operation 'Market Garden'. The 1st Polish Parachute Brigade based in Stamford and the British 1st Airborne Division had joined forces with the American 82nd Airborne Brigade. The operation proved to be a major disaster and many of the paratroopers did not survive, an event commemorated by many plaques in Rutland churches. The plaque in front of Station Headquarters at Cottesmore reads; 'May the memory of comradeship sown in the skies of Europe forever be as green as the fields of Cottesmore'.

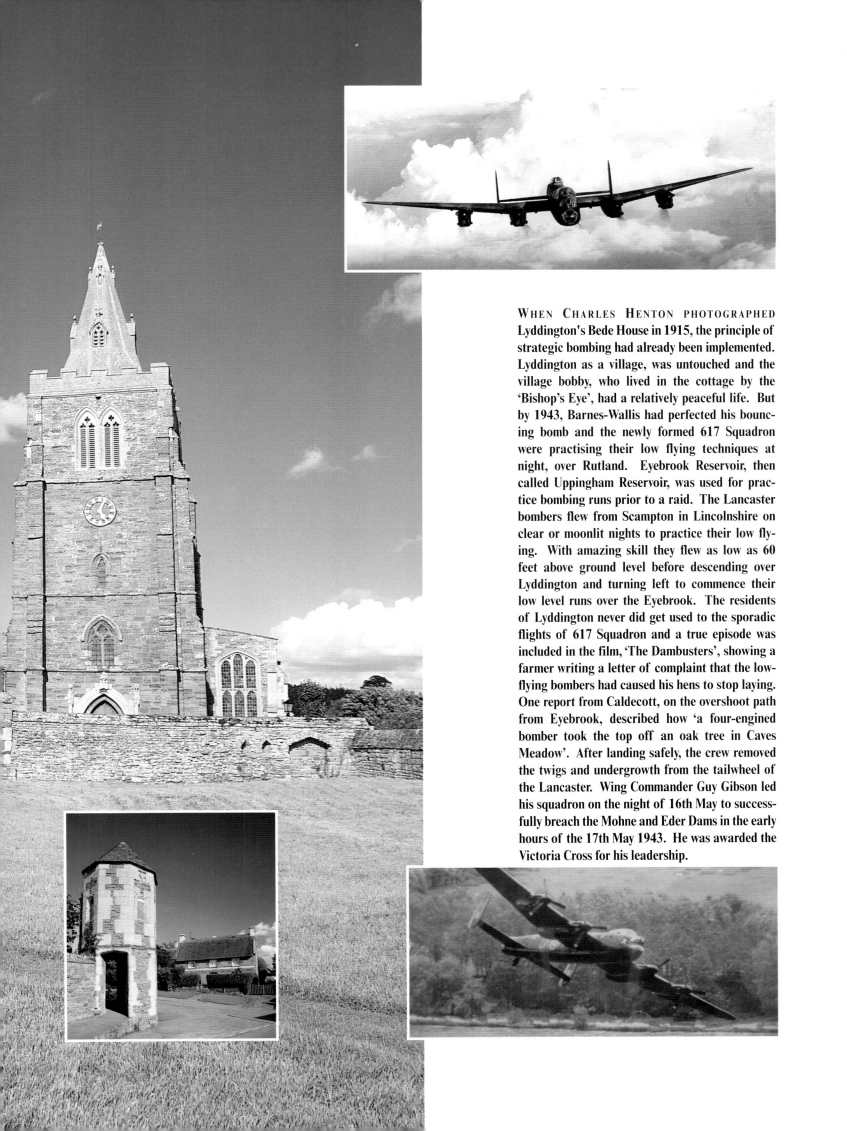

WHEN CHARLES HENTON PHOTOGRAPHED Lyddington's Bede House in 1915, the principle of strategic bombing had already been implemented. Lyddington as a village, was untouched and the village bobby, who lived in the cottage by the 'Bishop's Eye', had a relatively peaceful life. But by 1943, Barnes-Wallis had perfected his bouncing bomb and the newly formed 617 Squadron were practising their low flying techniques at night, over Rutland. Eyebrook Reservoir, then called Uppingham Reservoir, was used for practice bombing runs prior to a raid. The Lancaster bombers flew from Scampton in Lincolnshire on clear or moonlit nights to practice their low flying. With amazing skill they flew as low as 60 feet above ground level before descending over Lyddington and turning left to commence their low level runs over the Eyebrook. The residents of Lyddington never did get used to the sporadic flights of 617 Squadron and a true episode was included in the film, 'The Dambusters', showing a farmer writing a letter of complaint that the low-flying bombers had caused his hens to stop laying. One report from Caldecott, on the overshoot path from Eyebrook, described how 'a four-engined bomber took the top off an oak tree in Caves Meadow'. After landing safely, the crew removed the twigs and undergrowth from the tailwheel of the Lancaster. Wing Commander Guy Gibson led his squadron on the night of 16th May to successfully breach the Mohne and Eder Dams in the early hours of the 17th May 1943. He was awarded the Victoria Cross for his leadership.

CHARLES HENTON TOOK HIS PHOTOGRAPH OF THESE young boys in front of Home Farm in 1913, just before WW1 and long before WW2 when the airfield at North Luffenham was built. Wing Commander 'Johnnie' Johnson DSO DFC, author of 'Wing Leader', was born in Melton Mowbray. He knew Rutland well and lived for a time in the Old Hall at Lower Hambleton. In late May 1942, Johnson and his 'winger' were scrambled on a cloudy evening to intercept a lone bomber over Leicester at 2000 feet. "We flew only a few feet above the ground and just below the cloud base. We raced and curved over the wolds of Rutland and occasionally I caught a glimpse of a squat gray tower of a village church. I had spent my boyhood in Rutland so I knew our exact position. Control called for the last time on the radio; 'Steer 350, Johnnie. Buster (go to max speed). You're very close.' We both saw the bomber at the same time and I pivoted my Spitfire on her wingtip and came round for my attack. Wisps of white smoke began to stream from one of the engines but Brown was hit by the German rear gunner. His hood was shattered and something struck his right eye. In great pain and half blinded, Brown put his damaged Spitfire down perfectly at North Luffenham. We never saw the German bomber again." Wing Commander 'Johnnie' Johnson DSO DFC.

This incident may also tie in with another reported over Belton when a Dornier dropped bombs and was reported to have shot down a Spitfire. After WWII, in 1947, North Luffenham was host to the Royal Canadian Air Force flying their North American 'Sabre' fighters. Later, it became the base for Thor missiles and a focal point of the 'Cold War'. Home Farm has now been tastefully restored as a private house.

LONG BEFORE THE FIRST AVIATOR TOOK to the skies, Amos Alexander, the Head Forester of the Clipsham Estate, was trimming the yew trees that lined the avenue leading to Clipsham Hall. Nearby, to the south of the village of Stretton, another major airfield was constructed and numerous bomber squadrons operated from Woolfox Lodge. The Ram Jam Inn and the Jackson Stops were popular drinking places with both aircrews and groundcrews; it was here on the oak beams that they chalked their last messages. The Jackson Stops takes its name from the local auctioneer but the story of the Ram Jam Inn is more complicated. A lodger at the Inn couldn't pay his bill but offered to show the landlady how mild and bitter beer could be drawn from the same barrel. He drilled a hole in a barrel in the cellar and invited the landlady to stick her finger into the hole to stop the beer from leaking. He then drilled another hole at the opposite side of the barrel and invited her to stop the flow from the second hole. Once the landlady was immobilised, he made his escape.

THISTLETON, MEANING THE VILLAGE OF THISTLES, was given its name by Anglo Saxon warriors in the 11th Century but it had been a significant location since Roman times. A magnificent Roman mosaic was found during ironstone mining but today, the mining is finished and the landscape is once more orderly. Crossing the fields is a formation of the Red Arrows on their run in to Cottesmore for an air display. Below them, boys wearing red shirts carry out their own aerobatics and loops on a haystack, while on the shores of Rutland water, two ospreys fly in their own immaculate formation to their nest.

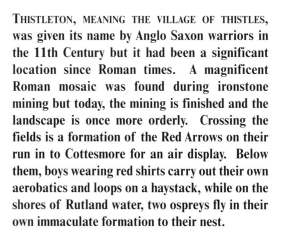

Chapter 5

Oakham County Town

THE WORD 'OAKHAM' IS DERIVED FROM THE SAXON words, 'Ocas House'. The first recorded Royal visit occurred in 1378 when Richard II visited Oakham Castle. According to local records William Flore, a wealthy wool merchant, was the leading townsman in Oakham at the time. The Flore's House Delicatessen and Café on High Street, now occupy the site of his old home. The next mention of Oakham was in 1375 when records state that a serious riot occurred between the men of Oakham, Langham and the inhabitants of Burley-on-the-Hill. The affair was bad enough to warrant calling out the Constable of Oakham Castle to restore order. Burley Church was desecrated and several men were wounded by arrows. In 1386, Roger Flore (William's son) is recorded as the Sheriff of Rutland. In 1390, the last mention of repair work to Oakham Castle occurs. The castle was in poor state of repair and from that time was neglected and fell into ruin over the succeeding centuries. Only the Great Hall remained; it continued to be used for the Assizes and the administration of other shire affairs until recent times. In 1396, Roger Flore, by then a wealthy merchant and member of the Staple of Calais, was elected MP for Rutland and was appointed Speaker of the House of Commons four times during his political career. His wealth enabled him to pay for the rebuilding of the spire of Oakham Church in 1425. In 1470, Edward 1V deposited the earliest of the surviving horseshoes in the Great Hall at Oakham Castle. In 1994, Ruddles' head brewer, Tony Davis, founded the Grainstore Brewery at Oakham and in 2003, The Prince of Wales made a visit on the 25th February to Grainstore Brewery and Oakham Castle.

A MARKET HAS BEEN HELD IN THE MARKET Square in the centre of Oakham since Henry III authorised weekly markets on Mondays and Saturdays in 1251. The modern view from Barclays Bank has hardly changed since then. Around the corner is the Buttercross with the stocks, first erected in the 16th Century when there were five crosses around the square but only two have survived. By 1252, Oakham was taking shape as a town. Richard, Earl of Cornwall, as Lord of the Manor, granted the people of Oakham the right to hold two fairs each year on the Feast of John the Baptist and the Feast of the Invention of the Cross. In 1256, court cases involving infringements of Forest Laws were first recorded as being heard at Oakham Castle. When Henton took his photograph in 1913, schoolboys from Oakham School were passing and stood still long enough to freeze their images forever. Today, mature trees create a deep shade. This part of the Market Place was originally known as 'The Parade' where the local militia carried out their drill practice.

ALL SAINTS CHURCH HAS AN EXCEPTIONALLY FINE 14th Century spire that can be seen as the dominating landmark on every approach to Oakham. The oldest part of the Church is the south porch, which dates to about 1190, although there is evidence of an earlier church mentioned on this site in the Domesday Book in 1086. The Church was further enlarged in the 13th Century when the nave aisles were widened and the chancel was extended. The tower and spire were completed in the 14th Century, including the square base of the 12th Century font bowl; the beautiful windows were added in the 15th Century. In 1616, Baroness Harrington presented a collection of 200 Latin and Greek folios to the library. The folios had been printed in London, Paris and Geneva in the early 16th Century. The Church also has a 13th Century Latin Bible. Catmose was originally the private home of the Right Honourable Gerard James Noel and Lady Augusta Noel and is now occupied by the restored Rutland County Council. The Rutland County Museum was originally the riding school of the Fencible Cavalry.

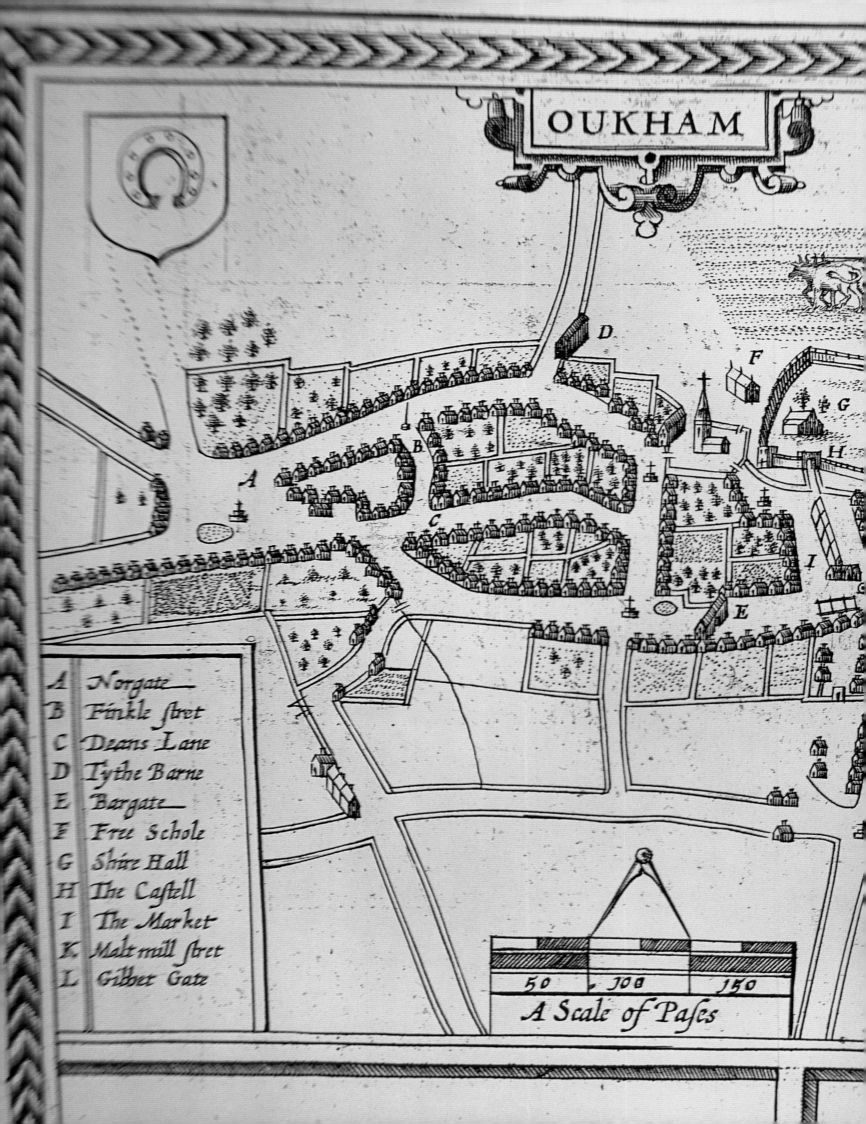

OUKHAM

A   Norgate
B   Finkle ſtret
C   Deans Lane
D   Tythe Barne
E   Bargate
F   Free Schole
G   Shire Hall
H   The Caſtell
I   The Market
K   Malt mill ſtret
L   Gibbet Gate

50   100   150

A Scale of Paſes

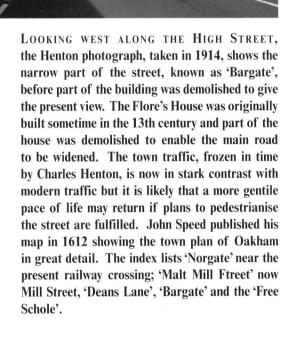

LOOKING WEST ALONG THE HIGH STREET, the Henton photograph, taken in 1914, shows the narrow part of the street, known as 'Bargate', before part of the building was demolished to give the present view. The Flore's House was originally built sometime in the 13th century and part of the house was demolished to enable the main road to be widened. The town traffic, frozen in time by Charles Henton, is now in stark contrast with modern traffic but it is likely that a more gentile pace of life may return if plans to pedestrianise the street are fulfilled. John Speed published his map in 1612 showing the town plan of Oakham in great detail. The index lists 'Norgate' near the present railway crossing; 'Malt Mill Ftreet' now Mill Street, 'Deans Lane', 'Bargate' and the 'Free Schole'.

THE AERIAL VIEW OF OAKHAM, TAKEN IN **1920**, is looking northwest over the town. In the foreground is Catmose House, today home of Rutland County Council, and in the lower left corner, the riding school of the Rutland Yeomanry, which is now the County Museum. Near the railway crossing is the cottage where the smallest man in England was born. Sir Jeffry Hudson, 'the least man of the least county in England' who figures in Scott's 'Peveril of the Peak', was born in Oakham in **1619**. At the age of nine, when only 18 inches high, he was taken into the Buckingham household at Burley-on-the-Hill where he was served up to Queen Henrietta in a venison pie. He became a firm favourite of the queen and was later to become her page. A painting by Van Dyke, still hanging in Petworth House in Sussex, shows the diminutive Sir Jeffery in the entourage of Queen Henrietta. He was knighted and had many adventures whilst travelling overseas, twice being captured by pirates. Today, a blue plaque denotes the cottage where Sir Jeffery once lived overshadowed by a monstrous truck rumbling and snorting its diesel fumes through the High Street.

HUDSON'S COTTAGE

Jeffery
Hudson

SMALLEST MAN
FROM THE
SMALLEST COUNTY
IN ENGLAND
1619 - 1682

OAKHAM TOWN COUNCIL

Chapter 6

Uppingham - Seat Of Learning

THE MASSIVE IMPOSING STRUCTURE OF THE **Victoria** Tower permits a glimpse into the courtyard of the modern Uppingham School. When the school was originally built and established, the Pilgrim Fathers have not even set sail for America. In 1584, Robert Johnson, son of a wealthy dyer, founded and endowed both Oakham and Uppingham Schools. He had pursued a successful career in the Church to become Chaplain to the Keeper of the Privy Seal and one of founding fellows of Jesus College, Oxford. Edward Thring, who arrived at the school in 1853 as headmaster, built upon the revolutionary thoughts that were set in place by the founder. He quickly developed the tiny school into a major educational institution, within ten years, increasing the number of boys at the school to more than 300. Edward was a pioneer in education and introduced many measures, including educational methods for the young that are now common throughout the world. His belief that education 'should be a full and rounded experience' is still referred to by modern educational physiologists as the fundamental rule that education should be an all-encompassing experience covering all aspects of the developing mind and body to advance with rational thoughts ensuring a balanced learning experience! Edward Thring was the founder of the 'Headmasters Conference', the first such conference being held at Uppingham in 1869. Old boys of the school served with distinction during many wars and skirmishes and have been presented with 4 Victoria Crosses and 267 Military Crosses.

BY 450 AD, THE ANGLO-SAXONS HAD SETTLED in northern and central England. Gradually, seven kingdoms emerged: - Kent, Sussex, Wessex, Essex, East Anglia, Middle Anglia, and Northumbria. Rutland was in the territory of Middle Anglia, which eventually took in adjoining areas to become the Kingdom of Mercia, based on Tamworth and Lichfield. Further south, in 1281, Edward 1 granted the Lord of the Manor of Uppingham the right to hold a weekly market on Wednesdays and an annual fair lasting three days. By 1299, Edward 1 had deforested the western two thirds of the Forest of Rutland, though Witchley Warren near Ketton were retained by the King. The Black Death broke out in 1348 and decimated the population, not only in the British Isles but also throughout Europe and the Middle East. Many of Rutland's 13 lost villages became deserted at this time. The High Street of Uppingham developed into the principal shopping thoroughfare of the town. The plough on top of the iron-mongers shop has sat in its position for over 100 years. Today, ladies run a charity stall in front of the Falcon Inn.

ARCHAEOLOGICAL EVIDENCE HAS BEEN discovered in various burial sites around Rutland. By 653 AD, Middle Anglia was ruled by Penda who converted to Christianity. Penda was succeeded by his son Peada in 654 AD and as King of Mercia, along with Oswy, King of Northumbria, founded Peterborough Abbey. Following King Alfred's decisive defeat of the Danes at Edington, England was divided along the line of Watling Street, Wessex to the south and the Danelaw to the north. Special provisions were made in the treaty for the area which became Rutland. The Danes agreed not to settle there and the area was partitioned between Danish administration based on Nottingham and Northampton. By Domesday the section administered from Northampton was Wapentake of Witchley, whilst the remainder, which had no common boundary with Nottinghamshire, was recorded as the Hundreds of Martinsley and Alstoe under Roteland as an appendix to Nottinghamshire. The town of Uppingham was built along the top of a long east west ridge, which had steep approaches from every direction. The dominant structure is the 14th century tower of the parish church of St Peter and Paul. Uppingham was originally a relatively small village but, during the era of coach and horses, it became a major crossroad. Here the east-west route from Leicester to Peterborough intersected with the north-south route between Nottingham and London leading to extensive development of the town, now the 2nd largest in the County after Oakham.

IN **1531 HENRY VIII** GRANTED THE PEOPLE of Uppingham the right to hold two fairs each year, one in March and the other in July. Through the centuries, the Market Place gradually became the focal point for a large variety of events. 100 years ago, it was the venue for the New Years' Eve meet of the Cottesmore Hunt and just recently housed a display of vintage motor cars. Almost 1000 years ago, in 'Domesday', we read of the King's Soc of Roteland (Soca Regis de Roteland) but the villages of present-day Rutland appear in the survey under either Northamptonshire or Nottinghamshire, showing that a considerable redistribution of territory has taken place since that time. It was not until King John's reign that Rutland was specifically called a county, when that monarch bequeathed it together with the 'town of Rockingham' to Queen Isabella. It seems probable that the district was known by the name of 'Roteland' for some time before it was raised to county rank. Uniquely, Rutland is the only shire not named after its principal town.

THE VIEW OF THE FALCON HOTEL, WITH ONLY TWO storeys, was recorded during the Edwardian craze for sending postcards. A new type of business was established in the High Street, that of the photographer. Mr Stocks opened his studio with an advertisement which declared; 'Mr Stocks makes a speciality of high-class portraiture and his studios are arranged to give the best lighting and modelling to the photographs, which together with careful finishing, go to produce a lifelike portrait. All kinds of outdoor photography, groups and animals taken by appointment.' Mr Stocks probably took the photograph of the meeting of the 'Suffragettes' from the first storey of the Falcon when, in 1907, Mrs Pankhurst addressed the crowd in front of the Queen Victoria Memorial. The portrait of a pair of Cross-Clydesdale Shire horses, owned and handled by Mr Tom Cliff, was taken almost 100 years later.

Chapter 7
The Villages of Rutland

BELMONSTHORPE LIES IN THE VERY EASTERN extreme of the county of Rutland where the fenlands of Lincolnshire begin. The village's name is derived from the term 'thorpe' meaning village and the name of the 12th century Le Bolour family. During his reign, Edgar, King of England, granted Rutland as dowry to his wife, as appears to have been the custom of the Anglian kings of Mercia. Later, Ethelred II, (the Unready) granted Rutland to his wife Emma and he attempted to buy off the Danish invaders by giving them large amounts of money raised through a tax called Danegeld. The Norman Conquest followed and William, Duke of Normandy, was crowned King of England. He graciously allowed Edith, the widow of Edward the Confessor and Harold to keep her lands until she died. In Edward the Confessor's will he left Rutland to Westminster Abbey which he founded. King William had Rutland divided, much becoming the King's land and Royal Forest subject to the notorious Forest Laws, whilst other parts were granted to Westminster Abbey in accordance with King Edwards's will.

BELMESTHORPE
20 02
BETULA JACQUEMONTII
GOLDEN JUBILEE

THE PARISH CHURCH OF PILTON IS JUST ONE OF the many fine churches of Rutland. The sheer diversity and numbers of churches in such a small county, which, until recently, had a relatively small population, often surprises visitors. Rutland has many fine buildings, not just churches but halls, manor houses and the more humble dwellings shown here, all displaying infinite variety both in style and detail. Whilst no architectural style is predominant, the result is not one of general disorder but rather a mellow and balanced scene where the beauty of the building stone provides the link. The abundant supply of excellent building stone weathers to a delightfully mellow grey in the case of the Oolite, and to a rich golden brown in the case of the ferruginous limestone. The early builders in the district were able to erect churches, houses and cottages to present the charming picture of today in a simple, rustic style. The symbols of the up turned horseshoe are everywhere and here in Pilton occupy an entire external wall of the old barn. The gentleman sitting outside his cottage is thought to be Harry Hawkes, a well-known breeder of donkeys.

EXTON, AN ANGLO-SAXON TERM MEANING 'AN OX farm' was first mentioned in 1185 as Exton Park. At that time, it was Rutland's largest park, encompassing almost 1,500 acres with a resident herd of 500 deer. Ironstone has been quarried in the Exton area of Rutland since the 1880s, but, at the end of World War II, the demand for steel to re-build Great Britain was increasing rapidly. In April 1949, work commenced to open a quarry at Exton Park on land leased by the Earl of Gainsborough. The approach railway was a siding from the Midland Railway near Ashwell and is now the site of the Rutland Railway Museum. Iron ore extraction commenced on a small scale until the huge 1400-ton dragline was assembled on site in 1957. The new machine was christened 'Sundew' after the Grand National winner that year. It was the largest excavator in the world, taller than Nelson's column in Trafalgar Square and was able to mine it's own weight of 1400 tons in one hour! By 1973, the Exton Park quarry was almost exhausted and it was decided that 'Sundew' would 'walk' across Rutland to a new quarry near Corby. The 'walk' started on the 19th June 1974 and 'Sundew', like her racing predecessor, performed in style, leaping 1 railway, 2 gas mains, 3 water mains, 4 rivers, 7 telephone lines, 10 roads, 13 power lines, and actually went through 74 hedges - a total distance of 13 miles - a true thoroughbred to the end. Today, 'Sundew' has been finally dismantled and Exton Park is now arable and pastureland again and it is difficult to tell that such a massive machine or the quarry, ever existed.

BRAUNSTON-IN-RUTLAND STANDS BESIDES THE RIVER Gwash on its route to empty into Rutland Water. The extensive farmhouses, cottages, church and its two pubs were built using the dark brown local marlstone. Originally, there were seven public houses in Braunston but today only the Old Plough and the Blue Ball remain in business. A pagan idol was found during restoration work at the church and is thought to be a Celtic 'Earth mother' figure, 2,000 years old. It now stands propped up at the back of the church, possibly the ugliest effigy in Rutland. The black Chrysler taxi of Mr Tim Norton had many important passengers. It conveyed the Prince of Wales on various occasions, Von Ribbentrop on his way to play golf at Luffenham Heath, and Herman Goering to the Cottesmore Hunt. The taxi was originally bought for £25/- in 1930 and was in service until 1967, having clocked up 531,500 miles, (855,183 kilometres).

A ROMAN KILN WAS FOUND IN A LIMESTONE quarry near Greetham. However, the Saxon word for village - 'ham' indicates that Greetham and surrounding villages such as Clipsham, Bytham and Witham were a major focus area for Anglo-Saxon settlements. Within the village of Greetham was Fountains Woodyard where a steam traction engine provided the power to drive a sawmill. Nearby, the Wheatsheaf Inn stood on the main track from Oakham to the Great North Road at Stretton. Once the village pump stood outside the Inn, which provided water for passing coach horses using the turnpike connecting Oakham with the Great North Road, now the A1. Today, the woodyard, the coach horses and the village pump have disappeared, the trees have matured but at the bottom of the garden, the stream still flows, a source of water that was the lifeblood of a steam traction engine.

MARKET OVERTON IS SITUATED HIGH ON THE limestone escarpment with extensive views to the west towards Teigh on the lower plain. Market Overton is one of the oldest villages in Rutland and, as its' name suggests, may have been the principal market town in Saxon times. The Romans settled here long before the Saxons and their buildings were used to build newer Saxon structures. During the ironstone mining operations in the 1906, gold, silver and bronze coins and artefacts dated around 600 AD were found. Isaac Newton grew up in the village in the 1640s, looked after by his grandmother. Isaac was educated at King's School in Grantham and legend suggests that the apple, which provided the clue to gravity, fell on his head whilst he was sitting in an orchard at Woolsthorpe Manor in Colsterworth. Isaac would have seen the stocks on the green in use during his childhood; they were last used in 1838. The village of Teigh sits on the plain below Market Overton, once surrounded by canals and railways. The focal point of this quiet village is the restored Church of Holy Trinity.

IN THE 7TH CENTURY, THE NIECE OF KING PENDA of Mercia, Saint Tibba and her cousin, Saint Eabba, were said to have lived in the village of Ryhall. Initially they were 'wild, hunting girls' but in later years became devout hermits. Legend tells us that the present church in Ryhall is built on the site of their cells. Saint Tibba was buried at Ryhall but in 936 AD, her body was exhumed and transferred to Peterborough where her official feast day is celebrated on the 6th March. Saint Tibba is acknowledged as the patron saint of falconers and wild-fowlers because of her early association with the chase. Today, a single lane bridge crosses the river into the village. Two public houses sit on either side of the main street leading down to the church and the square where a tree was planted to commemorate the 80th birthday of Queen Elizabeth, the Queen Mother.

THIS SYCAMORE TREE
COMMEMORATES THE 80TH BIRTHDAY OF
H.M. QUEEN ELIZABETH
THE QUEEN MOTHER 4TH AUGUST 1980
REPLACING AN EARLIER TREE
PLANTED HERE TO MARK
THE CORONATION OF
H.M. QUEEN VICTORIA IN 1837

THE SQUARE

TICKENCOTE AND TIXOVER ARE BOTH SITES of exquisite Norman churches. St Peter's Church at Tickencote has an impressively large Norman arch with a vaulted chancel and is situated as a focal point to the village west of the A1. The carvings on the arch show heads of kings, cats, leaves, foxes and faces, some beautiful, some rather grotesque. The massive Norman tower of the St Mary Magdalene church at Tixover now stands in isolation with the village almost 1 mile away. This is not by design but the outcome of the Black Death when many of the villagers perished; their corpses were buried in a mass grave close to the church. The abandoned cottages soon became neglected and were eventually destroyed. The remaining cottages now stand with an elevated and unrestricted view over the River Welland.

THE AMERICAN POET HENRY WADSWORTH
Longfellow made two long visits to England and,
having paid his respects to his hosts, visited many
areas of central England, walking and talking
with 'ordinary folk' whilst staying at humble
inns and taverns. It is believed that he used this
idyllic location as the inspiration for his classic
poem written in 1842. Today, the chestnut trees
have grown larger and the fishponds have been
flooded by Rutland Water but the gates to Burley
stand unchanged and industry continues in the
guise of an upholsterer's shop.

'Under a spreading chestnut-tree,
The village smithy stands;
The smith, a mighty man is he,
With large and sinewy hands;
And the muscles of his brawny arms
Are strong as iron bands.

His hair is crisp, and black, and long,
His face is like the tan;
His brow is wet with honest sweat,
He earns whate'er he can,
And looks the whole world in the face,
For he owes not any man.

Week in, week out, from morn till night,
You can hear his bellows blow;
You can hear him swing his heavy sledge,
With measured beat and slow,
Like a sexton ringing the village bell,
When the evening sun is low.

And children coming home from school
Look in at the open door;
They love to see the flaming forge,
And hear the bellows roar,
And catch the burning sparks that fly
Like chaff from a threshing-floor.

He goes on Sunday to the church,
And sits among his boys;
He hears the parson pray and preach,
He hears his daughter's voice,
Singing in the village choir,
And it makes his heart rejoice.

It sounds to him like his mother's voice,
Singing in Paradise!
He needs must think of her once more,
How in the grave she lies;
And with his haul, rough hand he wipes,
A tear out of his eyes.

Toiling,--rejoicing,--sorrowing,
Onward through life he goes;
Each morning sees some task begin,
Each evening sees it close.
Something attempted, something done,
Has earned a night's repose.

Thanks, thanks to thee, my worthy friend,
For the lesson thou hast taught!
Thus at the flaming forge of life
Our fortunes must be wrought;
Thus on it's sounding anvil shaped,
Each burning deed and thought.'

**Henry Wadsworth Longfellow
(1807 to 1882)**

IN 1817, THE POET JOHN CLARE CAME FROM Helpston to Great Casterton to work as a lime burner for Mr Wilders of the New Inn (now the Crown). It was here he met Patty Turner who, in 1820, became his wife when they were married at Great Casterton Church. His first book of poetry, 'Poems Descriptive of Rural Life and Scenery' was published in London under patronage of the Marquess of Exeter at Burghley. His later impressions were recorded in 'Sonnet to the River Gwash'. The Elergy on the ruins of Pickworth, Rutlandshire, was hastily composed and written with a pencil on the spot. One verse in particular describes the scene as he saw it then:

'Ye scenes of desolation spread around,
Prosperity to you did once belong,
& doubtless where these brambles claim the ground,
The glass once flowd to hail the ranting song.'

John Clare, 'The Peasant Poet', (1793 to 1864).

Chapter 8
Tourism & Sports

VINTAGE CARS CROWD AROUND THE 'MARQUIS OF Exeter's Arms' in Borrowden. Thomas Cook was an itinerant rural Baptist Minister who married Marianne Mason in St Peter's Church in Borrowden on 2nd March 1833. A plaque at West Farm in Borrowden now marks her former home. They set up home in the village where Thomas worked as a cabinet-maker. The couple moved to Market Harborough where on the 9th June 1841, Thomas had a flash of inspiration about the use that could be made of the new railways. On the 5th July 1841, the first ever day-trip on the railway was made when he took a party of travellers from Leicester to a temperance fete at Loughborough. This was the founding moment of Thomas Cook & Son, now one of the world leaders in sophisticated tourism.

On Monday, the 21st August 1916 at precisely 1.37 pm, Charles Henton took his photograph of the pond at Barrowden with the public house, 'The Marquis of Exeter's Arms' in the background. Charles Henton was born in Leicester in 1861, trained as an artist before mastering the 'new' art of photography. When he died in 1924, aged 63, he left an impressive collection of photographs and paintings, which are now housed in the Leicester Archives. At nearby Thorpe-by-water, a mighty vintage Bentley is prepared to take part in a modern race at Donnington Race Track. Equally mighty was the village miller, a Mr Goodwin, who was renowned for his ability to carry an 18 stone (more than 300 Kg) sack of flour all the way to Lyddington.

CRICKET IS PLAYED WITH VIGOUR ON THE PRISTINE grounds of Oakham School. It has been played in the villages of Rutland since the 1700s. At Burley-on-the-Hill, the Earl of Winchilsea, George Finch, the 9th Earl of Winchilsea laid out one of the first cricket pitches. His love and interest in the game led him to become the prime mover in the foundation of the MCC in 1787. He was a very strong man who played with a bat weighing 4 pounds, almost twice as much as a normal bat. He played his last match, aged 64, in 1816, just ten years before his death.

Only 3 kilometres to the south of Oakham is the village of Brooke, the original site of Brooke Priory built in 1163, believed to have been the only monastic house in Rutland. After the suppression of the monasteries by Henry VIII, it was bought by the Noel family who in 1549 built a large Elizabethan mansion close by. Today all that remains of the old priory is the dovecote but it is still a favourite place for walkers who enjoy the peace and tranquillity of the area. In the 19th Century, a rare treasure was found in a cellar. This was small gilt and cloisonné enamel casket dating from the 13th Century and it is now on display in the Rutland County Museum.

LONG BEFORE SAILING ARRIVED ON THE NEW SHORES of Edith Weston, the village had been named after Queen Edith. In line with tradition this royal lady received 'Roteland' of which Edith Weston was part, as a gift from her husband, King Edward the Confessor. The stump of the market cross indicates the centre of the village near King Edward's Way, yet another reminder of the village's royal connections. The village contains many fine buildings including St Mary's church built around 1170 AD and the old Rectory built in 1626. A tunnel was found beneath the 'Domesday Oak', when workmen were searching for water in 1964. The tunnel was said to have originated in the Old Hall and continued to Normanton Hall. There has been much speculation about its purpose. Charles Henton photographed the parsonage nearly ninety years ago, in 1915. It has changed little since that time. Sailing and fishing are now major pastimes off Edith Weston and even the old Oakham canal has a fair share of pike.

MANTON STANDS ON A HIGH POINT OF
Rutland where the main turnpike road from
Uppingham to Oakham once ran past the Horse
& Jockey pub. Far beneath it the railway tunnel
still runs. Just south of the village, the Leicester-
Oakham-Stamford line met the line from Kettering,
which passed over Seaton Viaduct. In the hectic
railway days of the 1870s, Manton became the
original destination for commuters simply because
it was possible to catch a train at Manton and be
in London-St Pancras a few hours later. The
Prime Minister at the time, the Yorkshire-born Mr
Asquith, lived at Manton Grange long before the
landscape was altered forever by the rising flood
of Rutland Water. Today, the village is by-passed
and the trains glide straight through the tunnel.
The Horse & Jockey, once a half way halt for the
coach service is now a major stopping point for
the formations of cyclists on the round-Rutland-
Water-ride.

Fox hunting became popular with the local gentry during the 17th Century and the open pastures of Cottesmore country were ideal places to follow this pursuit. Tom Noel of Exton was born in 1705; he is thought to be the originator of the Cottesmore Hunt and has been described as one of the greatest personalities ever to chase a fox. He had an undistinguished political career as MP for Rutland but in 1732, Tom Noel published the first book ever written on fox hunting.

Near Cottesmore is the hamlet of Barrow, the smallest village in the smallest county in England. In 1788, Sir William Lowther brought foxhounds down from Westmoreland and built new kennels for them at Exton. The Exton Hunt of 'Old Noel's Hounds' later became known as the Cottesmore Hunt. Over the years, the Hunt met at both Barnsdale Hall and Barnsdale Lodge. The Hall and the Lodge are now both unique hotels with fine restaurants. Among the open woodland of Barnsdale, modern 'A' frame, dark wood lodges have been discreetly positioned, almost invisible to passing cyclists and walkers enjoying the beauty of Rutland Water. The avenue of trees leading to Barnsdale Lodge is still known as 'The Queen of Bohemia's Ride' after the daughter of King James I, Princess Elizabeth, stayed for a while at Exton Park before marrying and becoming Queen of Bohemia.

WING MAZE IS DECEPTIVE IN APPEARANCE, IT DOESN'T conform to the modern idea of a maze, a place of high hedges, secret places and puzzling turns. This type of maze dates to medieval times and similar mazes are to be found elsewhere in England. The true purpose of the Wing maze was one of penitence whereby the devout would complete the wondering of the maze on hands and knees, head down, saying and repeating prayers at certain points before finally reaching the centre.

The cultured sport of bowling also requires a certain amount of head-down concentration to achieve a delicate and sometimes vigorous conclusion to a game. The main street of Wing has hardly changed since Henton's day, except that the ivy has gone from the cottage.

Chapter 9
Natural History & Culture

PANDION, THE KING WHOSE DAUGHTERS TURNED into birds is a character of myth. Pandion haliaetus, or the Osprey, on the other hand is a real tale of how the prince of birds has been raising its young at Rutland Water at the Nature Reserve at Egleton. Between 1997 and 2001, after an absence in England of over 50 years, the Rutland Osprey Project moved 64 chicks from a stronghold in Scotland to Rutland. Success arrived in 2003 when 5 chicks were born. The project, co-ordinated by Tim Appleton, was photographed by David Slater who quotes;

'My first sight of an Osprey was above Rutland Water. The majesty of this large brown and white bird with piercing yellow eyes, slow graceful flight, powerful broad wings some 1.5 metres across, flying over the mirrored water just after dawn was spellbinding. It circled the lake before plummeting into the water feet first, powerfully regaining the air with a gasping trout in its talons. I was privileged to photograph the birds in 2004 with Tim's help. The male in flight above the nest is 08(97), or number 8 from the 1997 trans-location. He returned in 2004 to attract this Scottish female on her return migration from Africa. They failed to breed, but 03(97) teamed up with female 05(00) to successfully rear 3 chicks. Two other Rutland ospreys produced the first ever chicks in Wales in 2004 to the credit to the Rutland Osprey Project.'

David J Slater, Wildlife Photographer.

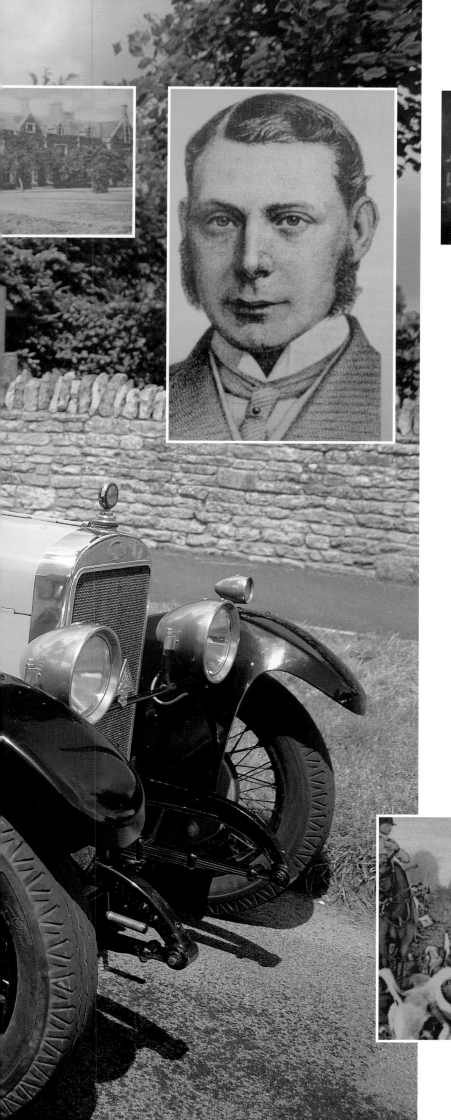

BARLEYTHORPE WAS THE HOME OF LORD Lonsdale, known as the 'Yellow' Earl due to his penchant of all things yellow, including his carriage, his car and even the livery of his servants. Amongst other pastimes, such as founding the Automobile Association and providing the 'Lonsdale Belt' for boxing, he was Master of the pack of hounds of the Cottesmore Hunt. Rutland became the centre of the foxhunting country and the social life that went with it. The season began in November with more than 500 horses attended by 250 grooms stabled in the surrounding area. The 'lovers of the chase' arrived, complete with ladies, chefs, food and wine. No expense was spared with individuals spending more than £3,000, a huge amount of money at that time, per season. As the popularity of hunting increased so did the population of Rutland. The sport required much human support with each huntsman needing 12 horses during the season costing more than £1,000 to upkeep. In the early 19th Century, in addition to Lord Lonsdale's Cottesmore pack, there was the Belvoir, the Quorn and the Atherstone. Hunting was hard on both horses and rider but the sport was considered 'good training and character building'. Lord Wellington said after the Battle of Waterloo that 'the best officers I had on the field of battle were the fox-hunters from Rutland and Leicestershire'. It appears that the majority of the population of Rutland and England still favour the sport of hunting.

DURING THE ROMAN PERIOD, TWO WELL-DEFINED
and clearly identified Romano-British camps
existed, one at Great Casterton, close to Ermine
Street or the Great North Road and the other at
Market Overton. Other smaller camps were built
at Hambleton, Whissendine, Ridlington and
Ranksborough near Langham and some recent
archaeological evidence has been identified with
this period. A bronze statute of Jupiter was found
near Ranksborough which is now in the British
Museum. A large number of Roman antiquities;
pins, brooches, coins and pottery have been
found at the other sites. It appears that there has
been a relatively large settlement at Hambleton,
probably due to its elevated position, coupled
with the easy access to water. A Roman pavement
was found at Tixover in the last century and
other Roman finds have occurred at Caldecott,
Casterton, Cottesmore, Lyddington and Seaton.
Hambleton was sub-divided into three almost-
separate villages; Nether Hambleton, which
disappeared beneath the rising water of Rutland
Water leaving the Old Hall of Lower Hambleton
at the waters edge and Upper Hambleton with a
new view.

LITTLE CASTERTON OR CASTERTON MINOR IS NOW well known throughout the world as the home to the open-air Shakespeare Company at Tolthorpe Hall. The original medieval Hall was built in 1550, re-built in the 1590s then 'restored' in 1867. In 1550, Robert 'Trouble church' Brown was born at Tolthorpe Hall. A pioneering nonconformist described as obstinate and dogmatic, he probably owed his survival to being a cousin of Lord Burghley, Principal Secretary of State and later Lord Treasurer to Elizabeth. In 1596, at Burley on the Hill, as part of Sir John Harrington's New Year's Day celebrations, the Chamberlains Men from London performed Shakespeare's play, 'Titus Andronicus' and Shakespeare himself is thought to have appeared on stage there. In 1977, the Rutland Open Air Theatre was built at Tolthorpe Hall and the Stamford Shakespeare Company staged their first productions during that summer. In complete contrast, a working weekend showing historical farm machinery, some maintained nearby by Ron Knight, takes place every autumn at Hall Farm.

A HILLTOP AT GLASTON IS THOUGHT TO HAVE BEEN a look out for the first inhabitants of Rutland. These early people lived by stalking and hunting and the remains of their successes have recently been unearthed. The oldest bones discovered were from mammoths and woolly rhinoceros. Local historians tell the tale of a circus elephant, a direct descendant of the woolly mammoth, trundling through Glaston in 1895 en route to be the major attraction at a circus, in Uppingham. Somehow the elephant fell down the well at the side of the road at Grange Farm. After much consideration and great local effort, the elephant was eventually rescued and was able to continue on its way.

Charles Henton photographed the 'Monkton Arms' in 1913 but the pub has now been totally renovated and re-named the 'Pheasant Inn'.

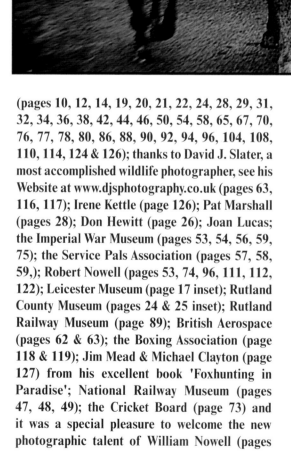

IN 1969, RUTLAND COUNTY MUSEUM OPENED IN Oakham and we made our first visit to Rutland, leaving the A1 and driving through Oakham then up to Royal Air Force Cottesmore to see RAF friends. We moved to Oakham in 1984 when our children were at Oakham School. Work started on this project in 1994. Many, many people were involved to make this project a success and we would like to thank the following individuals, companies and government departments; Viscount Campden; Carl Harrison, Sherry Nesbitt and all the team at the Leicester Archives; Sara Levitt and her team at Leicester Museums; Mr Simon Davies and the team at Rutland County Museum and especially Councillor David Richardson who kindly wrote the foreword.

It was a pleasure to collect the many excellent postcards dating from the early 20th century, taken by such photographers as Mr W. Stocks of Uppingham, Mr K. Bristow of Langham and Mr S. Cooke of Hambleton and to be able to publish some of their excellent photographs. The Charles Henton Collection, now housed in the Leicester Archives deserves special mention; Charles roamed around Rutland and noted the exact times and dates that he took his photographs. Having traced his path, I know that he was obviously a determined, patient professional photographer;

(pages 10, 12, 14, 19, 20, 21, 22, 24, 28, 29, 31, 32, 34, 36, 38, 42, 44, 46, 50, 54, 58, 65, 67, 70, 76, 77, 78, 80, 86, 88, 90, 92, 94, 96, 104, 108, 110, 114, 124 & 126); thanks to David J. Slater, a most accomplished wildlife photographer, see his Website at www.djsphotography.co.uk (pages 63, 116, 117); Irene Kettle (page 126); Pat Marshall (pages 28); Don Hewitt (page 26); Joan Lucas; the Imperial War Museum (pages 53, 54, 56, 59, 75); the Service Pals Association (pages 57, 58, 59,); Robert Nowell (pages 53, 74, 96, 111, 112, 122); Leicester Museum (page 17 inset); Rutland County Museum (pages 24 & 25 inset); Rutland Railway Museum (page 89); British Aerospace (pages 62 & 63); the Boxing Association (page 118 & 119); Jim Mead & Michael Clayton (page 127) from his excellent book 'Foxhunting in Paradise'; National Railway Museum (pages 47, 48, 49); the Cricket Board (page 73) and it was a special pleasure to welcome the new photographic talent of William Nowell (pages

21 inset, 22, 24, 26 sunset, 28/29-main picture, 32, 33, 37 inset, 41 inset and the portrait of the authors). For those interested in the technical aspects, I used a Mamiya RZ Professional with 40mm lens using exclusively Fuji Provia and Velvia rated at 160 ASA.

Thanks also to the anglers at Eyebrook Reservoir, Alan, Zena and Robin Doyle, Andrew Parsons and Steve Bell; David & Claire at the Old Plough at Braunston; Nigel Moon and his mother at Whissendine; Beryl Duce & Marjorie Keetley for their research, Val & Andrew Barrett in North Luffenham, Robert Bingley at Wing; Mr & Mrs Noel Burford at Greetham; John & Chris Grimmer in Oakham, Chris Lawton at Rutland Falconry; Steve Winston the postman; John Dalby the gamekeeper in Seaton; Ron the builder & Ian the hairdresser in Oakham; 'Bronco' Lane in South Luffenham; Ron Knight and Tom Cliff of the Ploughman's Society and the many people of

Rutland who allowed me access to their property to take photographs. Special mention needs to be made about the enthusiasts who gather old books, maps and especially old postcards; Simon Warner of LTS Books (page 45 inset); the Black Cat Bookshop in Leicester (pages 45, 47, 52); and especially Patricia, Naomi and Marcus at St Mary's Bookshop in Stamford (FEP, pages 43 inset, 70 inset).

Thanks to the unsung support of Marc & Patrick now in Oxford; Robert, Kerri, William and newly arrived Max in Houston plus Nicholas in Washington; lastly, thanks to our design and production team in Dubai; Robert, Simone and young Isa.

Finally, the people who made this project feasible; this book could not have been published without the support and encouragement of Peter Weller, David Bagshaw and Danny Daniels of Castle Cement, Ketton, part of the Heildelberg Cement Group.

Our thanks to you all.

John & Christine Nowell,
Oakham, Rutland.
27th November 2004

Published with the support and encouragement of: